*For Jean
Thank for your belief
in my work!
Claudia*

Claudia DeMonte

1976 – 2000

Published by the Department of Art, University of Maryland, College Park

ISBN #0937123404
Library of Congress #00-106867

Flint Institute of Art

Rosemont College

Islip Art Museum

Tucson Museum of Art

Brenau University

Ludwig Foundation of Cuba

COVER
Female Fetish: Shoe, pewter on wood, 7"h x 8"l x 3 1/2"d, **1996**

Printed in China
©2000 Claudia DeMonte. This book may not be reproduced without the author's written permission

Female Implements: Serving Objects:
#5 13"h x 5" 3/4" w x 2"d Collection of Lily and Philippe Staib
#9 9"h x 4 1/4"w x 3 1/2"d Collection of Ann Delaney
#6 11"h x 6" w x 2"d, Collection of Lily and Philippe Staib, bronze
1995

Claudia DeMonte: To Curate the World

[curate: to organize, to oversee, to take care of]

Nearly everyone has experienced it at some time or other. While shifting an unwieldy old chifforobe or stripping away some ghastly wallpaper, they appear…those indelible pencil marks on the wall, scratched at irregular intervals. Were they not inscribed and dated, the aggregate might appear to the art historical eye to be an early Sol Lewitt wall drawing. Yet, this composite is something far more personal and precious since it represents the often ad hoc familial recording of time, each superimposition of a line noting the passage of time, growth and maturity; each child placed against his/her sibling to see how they "measure up;" the entire vignette as it composes itself on the retina of memory an ideal subject for Norman Rockwell!

I don't know whether the Italian-American De Monte Family of Astoria, Queens practiced this particular intimate ritual. If they did not, young Claudia surely must have known about this American propensity for sizing up whether it be against one's friends or foes, or merely against the norm, since it became the leitmotif for her entire career: let's label it: "Claudia, Measure for Measure," not surprising for someone who was branded the "tallest girl in Queens!" Bolstered by her "passionately liberal" parents, Claudia was encouraged to think that one day a woman would be elected President of the United States and that "that woman could be me." "At thirteen, I decided that I didn't want to be president."

Yet, as in all true blue American success stories, the gawky, teenage "presidential candidate" becomes just-the-perfect-size for a fashion model…off she goes to Manhattan! Funny how a different calibration can lead to a far different assessment. But thus far the story is not so special, maybe it's even typical - ugly duckling-turning into-a-swan right in front of the camera. It's the American telegenic way, after all, isn't it? Yet, presidential stock or not, Claudia was clear on one thing, one very important thing: "women take care of the world."
Taking care of the world, for artist Claudia De Monte literally has meant that she continues to traverse its circumference, recording its wonders, the activities of other women, other women artists, who, like her, continue to "curate" their own lives and modulate and moderate the lives of those who dwell with them.

To this point, most of the art works, which she has produced since the early nineteen seventies, have dealt with the minutia of life, those things that "we do everyday that no one cares about." Things which no one cares about, but which everyone remembers and recognizes when they are reflected in the mirror of art. Everyday things which when accumulated, analyzed, and counted up, make us question just how we stack up. Have we spent too much time on this or not enough? Where has the time gone? Do these stupid little things really amount to a hill of beans? What is more important than a hill of beans especially to those women who count, cook, and covet them for those that they take care of. As early as the 1976 exhibition "Five plus One" at the Corcoran Gallery of Art in Washington, D.C., De Monte filled one wall with black and white photographs, which documented her performing everyday tasks. Another wall, hung salon-style, was filled with "things" emblazoned with her name. Someone cared and took care. The message: these petits riens are hers, goddammit! "Everything that I make is small, something that you can get close to, can hold near to you." Whether the small tabletop ceramic odalisques (1986) or the luxuriant fetishes (1997) or the bronze implements which reference the artist's own body (1996), each is redolent of its maker and carries the sense of a job-well-done, proclaiming to the viewer, 'if I were not needed, I would not have been made!'

According to Claudia De Monte everything counts in a world where everyplace is home to somebody. As she has traveled the world either in her art dreams where she levitates as St. Claudia the early Christian saint-non-saint or aboard a Boeing 747 racking up the mileage points, Claudia frequently asks herself the question, "Where is Home?"

Claudia DeMonte: To Curate the World

"I frequently wake up and don't know where I am?" Is she Escaping from Rome as in the title of 1982 series or merely seeing what is to be seen? Having grown up in her beloved Astoria where "everybody is from someplace else," the world as a concept never seems neither large nor strange, but merely navigable and eminently condensable, something to be packed up and put into a knapsack! All of De Monte's art objects have a numinous presence appearing more found then academically fashioned, a quality towards she strives. "I love to look at things that had to be made. Their makers had no choice but to make them." A loft filled with naïve/outsider art collected by De Monte and her husband, artist Ed McGowin, over the last twenty-five years, supports her assertion. About the artwork, which compels her, De Monte comments, "It is very intimidating to me as a formally trained artist to stand in front of a folk art work." Standing in her home, glancing back and forth between her own creations and those of artists from far-flung exotic places like Mogadishu and Bangkok, it is, at times, almost impossible to separate the two, each beguiling us with its utter intensity and shamelessly naïve artistry. Not surprisingly, saints and shamans are native to both De Monte's and outsider artists' canon. Both believe in the mythical creatures, mostly female who assist us mere mortals as we live our lives and take care of others in those simple ways that humans do.

That then is Claudia De Monte, a woman, a doer, a maker of simple and precious things, and artist of the rarest simplicity and honesty, a soul searching the world for more meaning, and upon finding it, curating for us, mere mortals, an astonishing moment of revelation.

Thomas Sokolowski July 2000

Claudia's Calendar
8 1/2"h x 11"w each
Collection of Franklin Furnace Archives, Museum of Modern Art, N.Y.
1976

Personalization Installation
18'h x 30'l
Corcoran Gallery of Art, Washington, D.C.,
1976

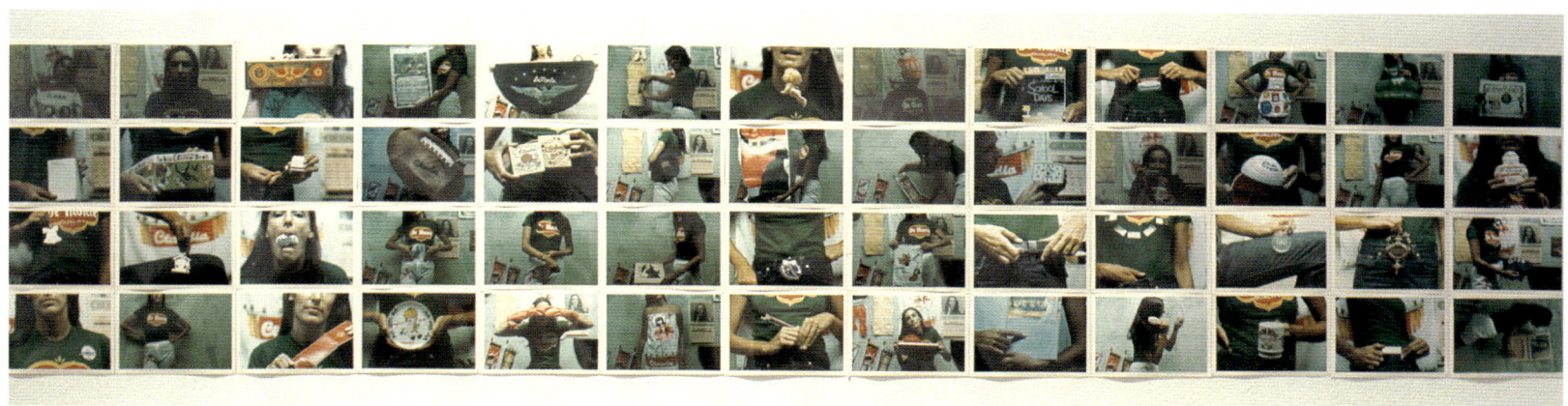

Personalization Part II
52 3"h x 5"w color photos
Corcoran Gallery of Art, Washington, D.C.
1976

Claudia in Washington D.C.
18 24" x 48" photoposters
Corcoran Gallery of Art, Washington, D.C.
1976

Trade Piece
100 mixed media photographs 8"h x 6"w each
New Orleans Contemporary Art Center
1977

Claudia Dolls
6"-9" acrylic on pulp paper, mixed media
Collection of Ruth Horiwich
1979

Installation, Droll Kolbert Gallery
acrylic on pulp paper, 30'l x 15'h, 3"d
New York City
1980

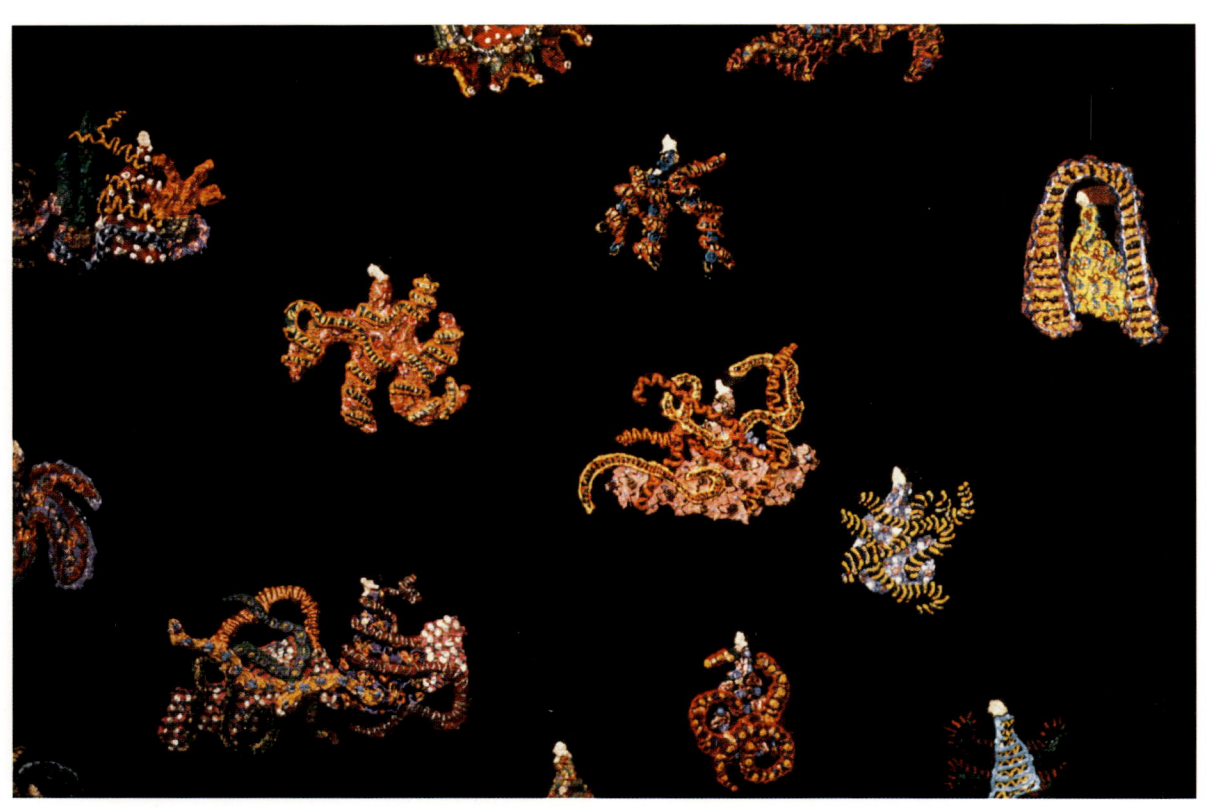

Astoria Fantasies
Installation detail, Queens Museum of Art, New York City
1981

Installation
acrylic on pulp paper, 15'h x 20'w x 3"d
Pam Adler Gallery, New York City
1982

Shrine to Learning
8'h x 6'w x 4'd, mixed media
Commission, N.Y.C. Dept of Cultural Affairs, Brooklyn Public Library System, New York City
1992

Animal Count
ceramic tile 30'l x 8'h
P.S. 51, Commission N.Y.C. Dept. of Cultural Affairs and
the N.Y.C. School Construction Authority, Richmond Hills, Queens, New York City
1994

The Shrine to St. Claudia
mixed media, 95" x 20" x 20"
Collection of The Brooklyn Museum, New York
1984

Icons
acrylic on wood
5"h x 81/2"w x 1"d, 6"h x 9"w x 1"d, 7"h x 9 3/4"w x 1"d
Collections: Vera List, Herb and Dorothy Vogel, Peaches and Ed Gilbert, 1985
1984

Claudia Changing Towels in the Bathroom
acrylic on pulp paper, 13"w x 10"h
Collection of Sue and Steve Gerson, 1984
1984

At Home and Abroad
acrylic and pulp paper on Gator Board, 93"h x 128"w x 3"d
Collection of Bob Rich
1985

Queens Commemorative Columns
acrylic on Gator Board, 48"h x 12"w x 1"d
Collection of the Queens Museum
1985

Odalisque after Matisse
acrylic on air dried clay, 8"h x 6"w x 6"d
Collection Mary Ann Tighe and David Hidalgo
1986

Odalisque after Rousseau
acrylic on air dried clay, 5 1/2"h x 9"l x 5"d
collection of the Museum of Modern Art, Salerno, Italy
1986

Odalisque after Gaugin
air dried clay, 3"h x 10"w x 4"d
Collection of Agnes Gund and Daniel Shapiro
1986

Odalisque after Matisse
acrylic on air dried clay, 8"w x 12"h x 7"d
Collection of Marcia and Steve Berini
1987

Objects of a Woman's Life Installation
ceramic and acrylic, 8'h x 6'w, 7'd
Barbara Gillman Gallery, Miami
1992

Shrines
Installation, Gracie Mansion Gallery, New York City
1989

right: Shrine to Africa
acrylic and pulp paper on wood, 15"h x 8"w x 6"d
Collection of Mr.& Ms. David Driskell

middle: Shrine to Paris
acrylic and pulp paper on wood, 15"h x 8"w x 6"d
Collection of Penny McCall

left: shrine to Florida
acrylic and pulp paper on wood, 15"h x 8"w x 6"d
Collection of Marty Marguiles
1989

Shrines to Florida: Alligator, Orange Slices, Flamingo
acrylic and pulp paper on wood, 15"h x 8"w x 6"d
1990

Who Made these things?
acrylic on board, 6'h x 25"w x 1"d
1990

Where's Home
acrylic and pulp paper, on board, 8'h x 6'w x 2"d
1990

The Luxury of Exercise
acrylic and pulp paper on board, 6'h x 6'w, x 2"d
1990

Female Fetish: Iron
pewter on wood, 9 1/2"h x 7"w x 5"d
collection of Gladys Nillson
1996

Female Fetish: Handbag
pewter on wood, 10"h x 11"l x 3"d
collection of Agnes Grind
1996

Female Fetish: Telephone
pewter on wood, 8"h x 6"w x 6"d
Collection of Zena and Michael Wieners
1995

Female Fetish: Teddy Bear
pewter on wood, 8" h x 10"w x 6"d
Collection of Patti and Gavin MacLeod
1996

Womens World
applique in collaboration with the Women of the Tibetan tent factory, 25 18" squares
Lhasa, Tibet
1996

Female Implements: Serving pieces

#13, 21"h x 3 1/4w x 1 1/2d
Collection of Barbara Johnson and Ruth Gresser

#15, 16"h x 3' 1w 1/2d
Collection of Dr. Hadassah Brooks Morgan

#14, 17"l x 2 1/2"w x 1 1/4d
Collection of Lily and Philippe Staib
1995

The Queens Dream
mixed media installation
2000

The Queens Dream, detail

Hand towel
Digital print on fabric, 12"h x 5"w
2000

Piede dei Miracoli
digital print on paper, 18"h x 11"w
collection of Carole Cole Levin
2000

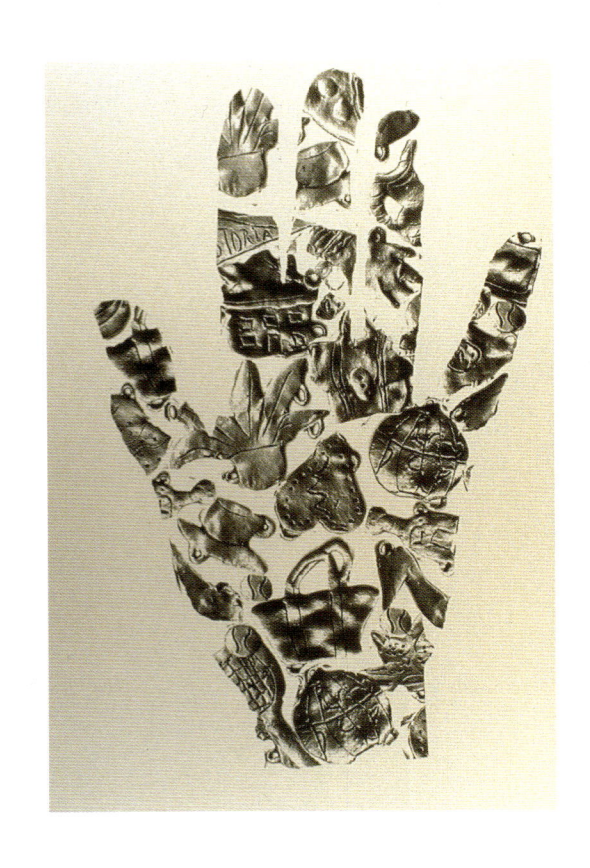

Mano dei Miracoli
digital print on paper, 18"h x 11"w
collection of Prince and Princess Abdullah bin Faisal bin Turki al Saud
2000

Claudia DeMonte

Born: Astoria, New York, August 25, 1947

SELECTED ONE PERSON SHOWS/PROJECTS/PERFORMANCES

2001 "Claudia DeMonte: Retrospective", Rosemont College, Pa.
Site Specific 2001, Islip Art Museum, New York
2000 "Claudia DeMonte" Flint Institute of Art, Michigan
"Women of the World: A Global Collection of Art", White Columns, NY
Flint Institute of Art, Michigan, University of Maryland Art Gallery,
Delta Axis, Memphis, Tn, Tucson Museum,Az, Brenau Un. Georgia
Mobile Museum, Alabama, Alexandria Museum, La., Museum of the Southwest, Texas
1999 "Female Fetishes", Gallery Liesbeth Lips, Rotterdam, The Netherlands
1998 "Claudia DeMonte: Retrospective", Chokladfabriken, Malmo Sweden.
1997 "Female Fetishes", Genkan Gallery, Tokyo Japan
"Female Implements"Silpakorn University, Bangkok, Thailand
1996 "Domestique", Leedy Voulkos Gallery, Kansas City, Missouri
"Female Implements: Serving Objects", Panorama Gallery,Winchester School of Art, Barcelona, Spain
1995 "Housewives", Xochipilli Gallery, Birmingham, Michigan
1994 "New Work", Barbara Gillman Gallery, Miami, Florida.
1993 "Female Fetishes", Nina Freudenheim Gallery, Buffalo, New York.
1992 "Objects of a Woman's Life", Jones/Troyer Fitzpatrick Gallery, Wash, D.C.
"New Work", Barbara Gillman Gallery, Miami Beach, Florida.
1991 "Claudia DeMonte", Gallery 86, Lodz, Poland
1990 "Claudia in the Tropics, Shrines and Amphora", Barbara Gillman Gallery, Miami, Florida.
1989 "Claudia DeMonte/Ed McGowin", Falcon Gallery, Riyadh, Saudi Arabia
"Shrines", Gracie Mansion Gallery, New York, New York.
1988 "Amphora", Jones/Troyer Gallery, Washington, D.C.
1987 "Odalisques"Nina Freudenheim Gallery, Buffalo, New York
"Odalisques", Gracie Mansion Gallery, New York, New York
"Her World", Brentwood Gallery, St. Louis, Missouri.
1986 "Windows", Grey Art Gallery, New York University, New York
1985 "Claudia DeMonte", Gallery 234, University of Wyoming, Laramie, Wyoming
"Claudia DeMonte", The Queens Museum, Flushing Meadows, New York.
"Claudia at Home & Abroad", Gracie Mansion Gallery, New York, New York

1985 "Claudia at Home with Her Religion", Joyce Goldman Galerie, Montreal, Canada.
"Claudia in Belgium", Gallery 121, Antwerp, Belgium.
"Claudia DeMonte", Stamford Museum, Stamford, Connecticut.
1984 "Claudia at Home with Her Religion", Gracie Mansion Gallery, New York,NY
1983 "Claudia DeMonte, Recent Work & Installation", Rathbone Gallery, Russell Sage College, Albany, New York.
1982 "Claudia DeMonte", New School for Social Research, New York, New York..
"Claudia DeMonte Installation", 500 Exposition Gallery, Dallas, Texas.
"DeMonte: New Work", Swope Gallery, Los Angeles, California.
"Claudia DeMonte", Shipka Gallery, Sofia, Bulgaria.
1981 "Claudia DeMonte", Miami-Dade Community College, Coral Gables, Florida.
"Claudia DeMonte", Marianne Deson Gallery, Chicago, Illinois.
"Claudia DeMonte", Marion Locks Gallery, Philadelphia, Pennsylvania.
1980 "Claudia DeMonte", Washington Project for the Arts, Washington, D.C.
"Claudia DeMonte", Fort Worth Art Museum, Fort Worth, Texas.
"Claudia DeMonte", Western Michigan University, Kalamazoo, Michigan.
"Claudia DeMonte", Memphis State University, Memphis, Tennessee.
"Claudia DeMonte", Mississippi Museum of Art, Jackson, Mississippi
1979 "Trade Piece", 80 Langton Street, San Francisco, California..
"Claudia DeMonte", Marianne Deson Gallery, Chicago, Illinois.
1978 "Trade Piece", American Cultural Center, Paris, France.
"Measuring Event", Franklin Furnace, New York City, New York.
"Trade Piece", Cranbrook Academy of Art Museum, Cranbrook, Michigan.
"Trade Piece", Baltimore Museum of Art, Baltimore, Maryland.
"Trade Piece", Contemporary Arts Center, New Orleans, Louisiana.
1976 "Five Plus One", Corcoran Gallery of Art, Washington, D.C.
"Process Art Trade: T-Shirts", Max Protetch Gallery, Washington, D.C.
1974 "Claudia DeMonte", Appalachian State University, Boone, North Carolina

SELECTED GROUP EXHIBITIONS

2000 "Extraordinary Things:A Study of Contemporary Art through Material Culture" University of Bridgeport Gallery, Ct.
"Continuous Fiction"Waikehe Community Art Gallery, Auckland, New Zealand
"The Really Big Shoe Show", City Museum, St. Louis, Mo.
1999 "Transcending Boundaries", Monarch Art Center, Tenino, Washington
"All God's Children Got Shoes", Miami-Dade Cultural Center, Florida
"Cats and Dogs", Jean Albano Gallery, Chicago, Illinois
"Revelations in Rubble", Walsh Gallery,Seton Hall University, So. Orange, N.J.
1998 "Contemporary Goddess", Augusta State University, Georgia
"Artists Sketchbooks" Archives of American Art, N.Y.
"Women in the Vogel's Collection, Brenau University Gallery, Gainsville, Fla.
"Fashion", Gallery K, Washington, D.C.
"20 X 500", 500 Exhibition Gallery, Dallas, Texas & The Art Center, Waco, Texas
1997 "Model Home"Stanley Picher Gallery of Art, Kingston University, Surrey, England
"Selections from the Permanent Collection" Vero Beach Center for the Arts, Fla.
"The Changing Face of Narrative, Islip Museum, Islip, N.Y.
"Works on Paper" Konin Museum and Poznan Museum, Poland

1996	"Splash" Monique Knowlton Gallery, N.Y.	1985	"New York - East Village Art Situation '85", Accademia Di Belle Arti Museo Di Arte Moderna Di Catanzaro, Italy
	"The Comic Depiction of Sex in Contemporary Art" Galerie Im Haus 19, Munich, Germany		
	"Homebodies" Nations Bank, Charlotte, N.C.		"Out of the Ooo Cloud: Artists Salute the Return of Halley's Comet", Edith C. Blum Art Institute, The Bard College Center, Annandale-on-the-Hudson, New York
	"Rose", Joyce Goldstein Gallery, N.Y.		
1995	"In Three Dimensions: Women Sculptors of the 90's", Snug Harbor Museum N.Y.		"The Doll Show: Artist's Doll and Figurines", Hillwood Art Gallery, Greenvale, N.Y.
	"A Childs Room" Fayerweather Gallery, University of Virginia, Charlottesville, Va.		"American Art: American Women", Stamford Museum and Nature Center, Connecticut
	"Shoes or No Shoes", Provincial Museum of Modern Art, Oostende, Belgium		"Group Show", Centro Culturale Arts, Rome, Italy
	"Hiroshima: From Me to You" Fukuya Gallery, Hiroshima, Japan		"Draw Your Own Conclusions", Joyce Goldman Galerie, Quebec, Canada
1994	"Thirty-something", The Fine Arts Museum of the South, Mobile, Alabama.		"Getting Off", Civilian Warfare, New York City, New York
	"The Aesthetics of Athletics" Wustum Museum, Racine, Wisconsin		"East Village at the au Centre", Centre Saidye Bronfman, Montreal, Canada
1993	"Artist Designed Jewelry", Museo Staile d'Arte Moderna, Arezzo, Italy,		"Doll Show", New Math Gallery, New York City, New York
	"Artists Books", Barbara Gillman Gallery, Miami Beach, Florida.		"Precious: An American Cottage Industry of the Eighties", Grey Art Gallery, New York University, New York
	"The Doll as Metaphor: The Image of the Doll in Contemporary Art", Haggerty Museum, Marquette University, Milwaukee, Wisconsin		
		1984	"Dolls and Other Effigies", New Math Gallery, New York City, New York
1992	"New York Painting, P.S. 1", New York.		"Artist's Books-Book Object", University of Oldenberg, Germany
	"International Biennial of Paper Art", Duren Museum, Duren, Germany		"Animals, Animals, Animals", Stamford Museum, Stamford, Connecticut
	"Woman as Protagonist", Goucher College, Baltimore, Maryland.		"The East Village Scene", Institute of Contemporary Art, Philadelphia, Pennsylvania
	"New York, New York", Galerie Liesbeth Lips, Breda, The Netherlands		"Installation", Gloria Luria Gallery, Bay Harbour Island, Florida
1991	"Selections from the Permanent Collection", Indianapolis Museum of Art, Indiana.		"Contemporary Triptychs", Bard College, Annandale-on-the Hudson, New York
	"10 Years for 2000, Cultural Experience", Centro Insular de Cultura, Canary Islands, Spain.		"Painting and Sculpture Today", Indianapolis Museum of Art, Indiana
		1983	" New York" New Gallery of Contemporary Art, Cleveland, Ohio
	"Ten Years/Arsenale", Museum of Modern Art of Salerno, Italy.		"The Cultural Object", Abaage des Premontres, Pont-a-Mausson, France
	"20th Century Sculpture from the Permanent Collection", Housatonic Museum, Ct.		"Video", Gallerie Watari, Tokyo, Japan.
1990	"Objects and Entities: Small Sculpture", Art Gallery, New Mexico State University.		"Bienal de Pontevedra", Pontevedra, Spain
	"Small Works", Xochipilli Gallery, Birmingham, Michigan.		"Falling Annual Videofestspiel", Odder, Denmark
1989	"The Last Picture Show", Gracie Mansion Gallery, New York.		"New York Terminal Show", Brooklyn, New York
	"World Fair Show", Queens Museum, New York City, New York.		"Sofa Size Paintings", Gracie Mansion Gallery, New York City, New York
	"Personal History/Fictitious Self", Evanston Art Center, Illinois	1982	"Installations", American Center of Artists. Paris, France
	"Contemporary Sculpture Works", University Art Gallery, SUNY at Albany, New York		New New York", Florida State University, Tallahassee, Florida and Metropolitan Museum of Art, Miami, Florida
	"American Art", Warsaw Museum of Modern Art		
	"New York Now", Sundsvalls Museum, Sweden. Travels to: the Sodertalje Art Gallery, Sweden; The Esbo Museum of Art, Helsinki, Finland; The Norrkoping Museum of Art, Sweden; and the Gothenburg Art Gallery, Sweden		"Collection of Dorothy and Herb Voge", State University of New York, Potsdam, N.Y. and Northern Iowa University
			"Energism: New York Art of the 80's", Arthur Roger Gallery, New Orleans, La.
1988	"Group Show", Kaess-Weiss Gallery, Stuttgart, West Germany..		"Invitational", Pam Adler Gallery, New York City, New York
	"RAJZ/Drawing 88", Pecsi Galleria, Pecs, Galleria, Pecs, Hungary..		"Installation", Soho Center for the Visual Arts, New York, New York
	"Homage to Hopper", Baruch College Gallery, New York City, New York.	1981	"New Visions", Larry Aldrich Museum, Ridgefield, Connecticut
	"Columnar", Hudson River Museum, Yonkers, New York.		"New Acquisitions", Miami-Dade Community College, Miami, Florida..
	"Diamonds Are Forever: Artists and Writers on Baseball", Norton Gallery, West Palm Beach, Florida. York City, New York;		"Approach/Avoidance: The Object in the Obsessive Idiom", Queens Museum, N.Y.
			"Libers D'Artista/Artist's Exhibition", Centre de Documentacio d'Art Actual, Metronom, Barcelona, Spain
1987	"4th International Review of Contemporary Art", Arsenali della Republica, Amalfi, Italy		
	"Intimate Environments" McIntosh Drysdale Gallery, Washington, D.C.	1980	"New Imagists", Alternative Museum, New York City (catalog).
	"The New York Scene", Gallery Liesbeth Lips, Amsterdam, Holland.		"Glitter", Kathryn Markel Gallery, New York City, New York.
1986	"Fetish Art - Obsessive Expression", Rockford Art Museum, Illinois.		"Painting and Sculpture Today", Indianapolis Museum of Art, Indianapolis, In.
	"Illuminations: The Art of Your Future", Arte et Industrie, New York City, N.Y.		"First Person Singular: Recent Self-Portraits", Pratt Institute Gallery, N.Y.
	"Saints and Sinners - Contemporary Responses to Religion", DeCordova and Dana Museum and Park, Lincoln, Massachusetts		"American Women Artists", Contemporary Art Museum, University of San Paulo, Brazil
			"Summer News", Droll/Kolbert Gallery, New York, New York
	"The East Village", The Fashion Institute of Technology, New York City, New York		"New Talent", Audrey Strohl Gallery, Memphis, Tennessee
	"NYC: New Art", Delaware Art Museum, Wilmington, Delaware		

1979	"By The Sea", Queens Museum, Queens, New York (catalog)	
	"Other Child Books", Warsaw Polytechnic Institute, Remont Gallery, Warsaw, Poland	
	"New Work, New York", University of Florida, Tallahassee, Florida	
1978	"Artists Books USA", New Gallery, Cleveland, Ohio	
	"Art Words/Book Works", Los Angeles Institute of Contemporary Art, California	
	"X International Encounter on Video", Tokyo, Japan	
1977	"American Narrative/Story Art", 1976-1977, Houston Contemporary Art Museum, Texas	
	"Projects and Proposals for the Seventies", Institute for the Art and Urban Resources, P.S.1., Long Island City, New York	
	"Time", Philadelphia College of Art, Philadelphia, Pennsylvania,	
	"VII International Encounter on Video", Fundacio Joan Miro, Centre d'Estudio d'Art Contemporani CEAC, Parc de Montjuic, Barcelona, Spain	
	"Memory", C Space, New York	
1976	"VI International Encounter on Video", Caracas Museum of Contemporary Art, Venezuela	
	"Liberation: 14 American Artists", Aarhus Kunstmuseum, Aarhus, Denmark	
1975	"Inaugural Exhibit", Washington Project for the Arts, Washington, D.C.	
	International Women Artists", Olympia International Art Center, Kingston, Jamaica	
	"DeMonte Price", Haitian-American Institute, Port Au Prince, Haiti	
1974	"19th Area Exhibition", Corcoran Gallery of Art, Washington, D.C.	
1973	"Queens Talent '73", Queens Museum, Flushing Meadows, New York	
1972	"Process Parkway, an on-site execution of commissioned art works", Philadelphia Museum of Art, Pennsylvania	
	"Maryland Annual Show", Baltimore Museum of Art, Baltimore, Maryland	

PUBLIC & CORPORATE COLLECTIONS

Academy of the Arts, Easton, Maryland.
Bass Museum, Miami, Florida.
Bellevue Hospital, New York.
Best Products, Virginia
Boca Raton Museum, Florida.
Brooklyn Museum, Brooklyn, New York.
Center for Fine Arts, Vero Beach, Florida.
Centrum Szfuzi, Warsaw, Poland.
Chemical Bank, New York.
Corcoran Gallery of Art, Washington, D.C.
Delaware Art Museum, Wilmington, Delaware
Exxon Corporation, New York
Franklin Furnace Archives, New York City.
Grand Rapids Art Museum, Michigan.
Housatonic Museum, Connecticut.
Hvidovre Art Library, Odder, Denmark.
Hyatt-Regency Hotel, Virginia.
Indianapolis Museum of Art, Indiana.
Konin Museum, Poland
Miami-Dade Community College, Florida.
Mobile Museum of Art, Alabama
Minnesota Museum of Art. St. Paul, Mn..
Mississippi Museum of Art, Jackson, Mississippi.

MTV, New York.
Museum of Art of Fort Lauderdale, Florida
Museum of Modern Art of Salerno, Italy
Museum Artystow, Lodz, Poland
New Orleans Museum of Art, Louisiana
New School for Social Research, New York
Otis Art Institute, Los Angeles, California
Patterson Museum, New Jersey
Prudential Life Insurance, Parsippany, New Jersey
Queens Museum, New York
Queensborough Community College, New York
Rich Products, Buffalo, New York
Siemens, New York
St. Lawrence University, New York
Stamford Museum, Stamford, Ct.
Sweenter Shoe Museum, Antwerp, Belgium
Tucson Art Museum, Arizona
Twentieth Century Fund, New York
University of Maryland, College Park, Maryland
University of Oldenburg, Germany
Warsaw Museum of Modern Art, Poland
Frederick S. Wright Art Gallery, University of California, Los Angeles, Ca.

GRANTS/AWARDS

1999	Anchorage Foundation of Texas
1998	Agnes Gund Foundation Grant
	Arts Development Committee, Anonymous Foundation Award,
1997	Distinguished Scholar Teacher, University of Maryland, College Park, Md
1989	New York Foundation for the Arts Fellowship, Sculpture
1985	Cite des Arts Residency, American Center in Paris
1983	Ariana Foundation for the Arts Grant
1977	Institute for Art and Urban Resources, P.S.1, Workspace, Long Island City, NY
1975	U.S. Representative, Sculpture, International Women's Art Exhibit, Olympia International Art Center, Kingston, Jamaica
1972	Mr. and Mrs. Howard Head Award, Maryland Annual Show, Baltimore Museum of Art, MD

COMMISSIONS

1998	New Mexico Arts, Socorro, N.M. Sculpture Commission
1997	N.Y.C. Dept. of Cultural Affairs, Queens Supreme Court Sculpture Commission, N.Y.C.
1993	Percent for Art Mural Commission, P.S. 51, Richmond Hills, Queens, Department of Cultural Affairs/School Construction Authority N.Y.C.
1992	Prudential Life Insurance Sculpture Commission
1990	Percent for Art Commission, Department of Cultural Affairs, New York City, Clarendon Public Library, Brooklyn, New York
1984	Hyatt Regency Hotels Commission, Crystal City, Virginia
1981	Prudential Life Insurance Mural Commission N.Y.
1972	Mural, Bladen Hall, Prince George's Community College, Largo, Maryland
1970	Mural, Astoria Park, Queens, under the auspices of the New York City Parks Department

ACKNOWLEDGEMENTS

This publication was made possible by the generous support of:

Agnes Gund and Daniel Shapiro

Hadassah Brooks Morgan and Thomas B. Morgan

Adam Solomon

Anthony Solomon

Zena and Michael Wiener

Book design, art direction, and digital production by:

John DiMarco